811.08 243719
B62 4.95

Blood of their blood

DATE DUE			

ST. CLOUD PUBLIC LIBRARY
GREAT RIVER REGIONAL LIBRARY
St. Cloud, Minnesota 56301

BLOOD OF THEIR BLOOD

An Anthology of
Polish-American Poetry

Edited by Victor Contoski

Paper Cuttings by Wieslawa Contoski

New Rivers Press 1980
in association with
The American Council of Polish Cultural Clubs

Copyright © 1980 by New Rivers Press, Inc. and the American Council of Polish Cultural Clubs
All rights reserved
Library of Congress Catalog Card Number: 80-81942
ISBN 0-89823-020-9
Book Design: C. W. Truesdale
Typesetting: John Minczeski

This book was created under the sponsorship of the American Council of Polish Cultural Clubs (ACPCC), Anna Chrypinski, president. The editor and publisher wish to thank this organization for its generous support and Mr. Kirkley Coulter for his enthusiastic interest in this project.

This book was manufactured in the United States of America for New Rivers Press (C. W. Truesdale, Editor/Publisher), 1602 Selby Avenue, St. Paul, Minnesota 55104 and the American Council of Polish Cultural Clubs, 6300 Lake View Drive, Falls Church, Virginia 22041, in a first edition of 1500 copies.

ST. CLOUD PUBLIC LIBRARY
243719

BLOOD OF THEIR BLOOD

8. Introduction by Victor Contoski
9. Acknowledgements

12. DOUGLAS BLAZEK
13. Poem On An Old Theme
14. The Puppet
15. My Paper Axe

16. CHARLES BUKOWSKI
17. The Meek Have Inherited
18. The Loser
18. Something

20. FRANK CEBULSKI
21. XXXII: Carthage
22. LXXIV
23. LXXXVIII: Orpheus And Eurydice

24. VICTOR CONTOSKI
25. Salt
27. Night On The Prairie

28. BILL (BOLES) COSTLEY
29. For Dad And The Factory . . .
30. *from* Kulik/Krrulik

32. WILLIAM DORESKI
33. Hancock Hill In Midwinter
33. Snowshoeing To Start The New Year
34. Estabrook County

38. STUART DYBEK
39. Vivaldi
40. Penance
41. The Knife-Sharpener's Daughter

42. DONALD FINKEL
43. Weeds
44. What My Head Is For
45. How Things Fall

46. JOHN GOGOL
47. Native American Desert
48. Native American Words
49. Untitled

50. TERRY KENNEDY
51. The Pillow
52. There Is No Metaphor For Hate
53. Holding On

54. LEONARD KRESS
55. Bobowa
57. The Coming Of Darkness In Istebna
58. On The Bus To Zakopane

60. KARL KULIKOWSKI
61. Music In Greenpoint

64. STEPHEN LEWANDOWSKI
65. Wind Before Dawn
66. Willows
66. Heron
67. Anton & Anna Lewandowski

68. JOSEPH LISOWSKI
69. Family Ties
69. For Years
70. On The Way Home

72. JOHN MINCZESKI
73. Our Lady Of Wheat
74. The Man With The Wooden Heart
75. A Man Is Following His Heart

76. ED OCHESTER
77. As You Leave
78. The Tower At The End Of The World
79. In The Library

80. MARK PAWLAK
81. *from* The Buffalo Sequence

84. PHIL PAWLOWSKI
85. Waltz In "A" Minor
86. Language Lesson
87. Kluski (Noodles)

89. JOHN PIJEWSKI
89. Burying My Father
90. My Brother's Deaf Daughter
91. Night Walk

92. JOHN CALVIN REZMERSKI
93. Grandfather
94. Second Marriage

96. MARTIN J. ROSENBLUM
97. "can't get back..."
98. "this winter..."
99. At Sunrise (The Skin)

100. JEROME ROTHENBERG
101. A Polish Anecdote "The Saint"
101. A Polish Anecdote "Victory"
102. A Gallery Of Jews

106. MAXINE SILVERMAN
107. Hair
108. A Comfort Spell
110. Missouri

112. BARBARA SZERLIP
113. Russia, 1931
114. Envoy From Houdini
115. Open Letter From Lola Montez

116. LAURA LOUISE ULEWICZ
117. *from* Notes Toward The River Itself

120. DIANE WAKOSKI
121. The Father Of My Country
126. The Singer

INTRODUCTION

The aim of this anthology is simple: to present a collection of good poetry by Polish-American poets writing at the present time. Readers of contemporary poetry, Polish-Americans, and even the general public will, I hope, find it of interest; for the more contact between poets and public, the better for both. Poetry, after all, still brings us beauty and wisdom, though twentieth-century poetry may do so in surprising ways. It helps us understand our lives.

The poets write of what they know or what they would like to know: William Doreski of the New England landscape, Ed Ochester of the differences between the ideal country of the heart and the real world, Joseph Lisowski of his immediate family, and Jerome Rothenberg of Poland in 1931. Though this is not by any means a thematic anthology, I must admit a personal fondness for poems about the Polish past, which the reader will find liberally sprinkled throughout the volume.

Poetic techniques reflect the time in which the poets live. Lulling rhythms and long, melifluous lines with regular rimes may say much of the leisurely, ordered life of the nineteenth century, but they say less of life in the twentieth. We are used to harsher, uneven, surprising events in our lives, and we find them too in the techniques of our poets. Martin J. Rosenblum's spelling, for example—"&" and "nite" for "and" and "night"—forces us to read his poems more quickly; they *thrust* their experience upon us. Many poets speak directly to us in a conversational tone, sacrificing beautiful language for immediate dramatic effect. Douglas Blazek's voice speaks to us directly in the tones of the American working man. But even the words of a straightforward conversation can make beautiful music, as when Maxine Silverman's father croons (note the soothing effect of the long *o*'s and *n*'s) to his grown daughter, "Better soon. Soon. Soon."

The poets themselves span the broad philosophical spectrum found in contemporary American poetry, from the emphasis on traditional Western European cultural values in the poetry of Frank Cebulski and William Doreski to the emphasis on the individual as the primary source of art as in Charles Bukowski. Between these extremes fall the rest of the poets. Diane Wakoski, Mark Pawlak, and Terry Kennedy strive to elevate their personal lives into myths. So do Martin J. Rosenblum, Joseph Lisowski, and Leonard Kress. Barbara Szerlip, John Gogol, and Laura Louise Ulewicz look for the universal less in their own lives and more in the life around them: Szerlip in historical figures, Gogol in American Indians, and Ulewicz in the life of the river. Of particular interest are the poets who treat their specific Polish heritage as a symbol of the past they hope to recapture in their attempts to understand the present—Jerome Rothenberg, Maxine Silverman, Phil Pawlowski, Karl Kulikowski, Stephen Lewandowski, and Mark Pawlak. Finally there are poets of fantasy and surrealism: Donald Finkel, John Minczeski, John Calvin Rezmerski, John Pijewski, and Victor Contoski. Yet even these writers who build fantasies do so on solid reality. Stuart Dybek sees Vivaldi in Chicago cupping a match against the wind. We respond to the marvelous wheat princess and the woman who enters a man's skin in John Minczeski's world because in it we recognize parts of our own.

I have applied two criteria to the selections: the poet's ancestors must have come from Poland, and the poet must write good poetry, as defined by the fallible taste of the editor. Thus I include poets whose ancestors belonged to the minorities that have shared the Polish land and contributed in their way to the diversity of Polish culture.

If only it were possible to present *all* Polish-American poets! Several have been omitted, however, either because I was unable to contact them, because I learned of their work too late to include it, or because of the limitations of my artistic taste. I have selected only poems that I understand and like. Many of them I love—and have come to love them more the more I read them. I hope the readers will share my affection.

I should like to thank Kirk Coulter for his enthusiasm and encouragement, C. W. Truesdale whose editorial suggestions helped give the book its final form, the ACPCC for its financial support of the project, and finally the poets themselves for their patience and understanding.

ACKNOWLEDGEMENTS

The editor would like to thank the poets for permission to reprint their poems. And special thanks go to the books and magazines in which the poems first appeared.:

Douglas Blazek: "The Puppet" in *Ironwood*; "Poem on an Old Theme" in *Loon*; "My Paper Axe" in *Exercises in Memorizing Myself* (twowindows: Berkeley, 1976);

Charles Bukowski: "The Loser" in *A Bukowski Sampler* (Druid: Madison, 1973); "Something" and "The Meek Have Inherited" in *Love is a Dog From Hell* (Black Sparrow, 1977);

Frank Cebulski: "Carthage," "LXXIV," and "Orpheus and Eurydice" in *Mediterranean Sonnets* (Oyez, forthcoming);

Victor Contoski: "Salt" in *Broken Treaties* (New Rivers, 1973); and "Night on the Prairie" in *Hanging Loose*;

Bill Costley: "For Dad and the Factory: Lynn River Works GE" in *The Newspaper*, Lynn, MA; "Kulik/ Krrulik" in *The Small Pond*;

Stuart Dybek: "Penance," "The Knife-Sharpener's Daughter," and "Vivaldi" in *Brass Knuckles* (University of Pittsburgh, 1979);

Donald Finkel: "Weeds" in *Poetry Now*; "What My Head is For" in *Iowa Review*; "How Things Fall" in *Kayak*;

John Gogol: "Untitled," "Native American Words," and "Native American Desert" in *Native American Words* (Tahmahnawis: Portland, Oregon, 1973);

Terry Kennedy: "There is No Metaphor for Hate," "Holding On," and "The Pillow" in *Durango* (The Smith, 1979);

Leonard Kress: "Bobowa," "On the Bus to Zakopane," and "The Coming of Darkness in Istebna" in *Tryst* (Lalka, 1976);

Karl Kulikowski: "Music in Greenpoint" in *Haiku, Senryu, and Poetry* (Gusto, 1978);

Stephen Lewandowski: "Heron," "Willows," "Wind Before Dawn," and "Anton & Anna Lewandowski" in *Inside & Out* (Crossing, 1979);

Joseph Lisowski: "For Years" in *Poetry View*;

John Minczeski: "Our Lady of Wheat," "The Man with the Wooden Heart," and "A Man is Following His Heart" in *The Spiders* (New Rivers, 1979);

Ed Ochester: "In the Library" in *Dancing on the Edges of Knives* (University of Missouri, 1973); "As You Leave" and "The Tower at the End of the World" in *The End of the Ice Age* (Slow Loris, 1977);

Mark Pawlak: part xi in *The Buffalo Sequence* (Copper Canyon, 1977);

John Pijewski: "Burying My Father" in *Durak*;

John Calvin Rezmerski: "Grandfather" in *ETC.* and in *An American Gallery*;

Jerome Rothenberg: "A Polish Anecdote 'The Saint', "A Polish Anecdote 'Victory'," and "A Gallery of Jews" in *Poland/1931*. Copyright © 1974 by Jerome Rothenberg. Reprinted by permission of New Directions.

Maxine Silverman: "Hair," "A Comfort Spell," and "Missouri" in *Survival Song* (Sunbury, 1976); "Hair" also in *Rapunzel, Rapunzel* (McBooks, 1980) and *Voices Within the Ark: Modern Jewish Poets* (Avon, 1980); "A Comfort Spell" also in *Pushcart III: Best of the Small Presses* (Pushcart, 1978 and Avon, 1979);

Barbara Szerlip: "Russia, 1931" in *Gallimaufry*; "Envoy from Houdini" and "Open Letter from Lola Montez" in *Sympathetic Alphabet* (Mother's Hen, 1975);

Laura Ulewicz: "Notes Toward the River Itself" in *Reinhabiting A Separate Country* (Planet Drum Foundation, 1978) and in *The Delta Current Calendar* (Delta Current, 1978);

Diane Wakoski: "The Father of My Country" in *The George Washington Poems* (riverrun, 1967) and in *Inside the Blood Factory* (Doubleday, 1968); "The Singer" in *The Magellanic Clouds* (Black Sparrow, 1970).

BLOOD OF THEIR BLOOD

DOUGLAS BLAZEK b. 1941

Douglas Blazek was born in the Polish section of Chicago, which became a lasting influence on his work. "Polish custom, Polish language were too far removed to have any immediate influence; but that creed of labor and the necessity to immerse oneself in the apple-urine bath of reality will never leave. A stoicism and grace in facing adversity, a determination to see things to their end, an acceptance of pain and discomfort, a humble disposition to life; these are the trademarks I associate with my Polish relatives and the community in which I was raised. Such a force of earth and blood! Such commitment to honest muscle and the pure graces of simple pleasures! These sons and daughters of immigrants who raised me gave profundity of spirit and decency of purpose. Because of this background, my poetry tries to keep its feet on the ground, its images tangible, its direction from the meat hook to the mouth."

He now lives and works in Sacramento. His latest book is *Exercises in Memorizing Myself* (Serendipity: Berkeley, 1976).

Douglas Blazek

POEM ON AN OLD THEME

Pain is making the sign of the cross
on its knees head bowed
murmuring to itself

nothing is wrong
yet my body is leaking away
pouring onto the floor
like sugar from a torn sack

the taste of myself has vanished
only the taste of you remains
brushing the inside of my mind
knotting its mystery to my breath
the way an animal sends its voice
into the belly of its young

my direction is toward cliffs
where I extend my desires over the edge
to see which become too heavy to hold

dreams stir beneath my face
cleaned of every promise
the way a swing moves
from the quick absence of a child

you left me so many centuries ago
you leave again over and over this moment
in each future you are always absent
yet the taste of you remains

Douglas Blazek

THE PUPPET

My young son carved a puppet
and placed it on the table where it lies sulking like a fetus
absorbing the radiation of our behavior

its face is a father's face
its hands capable of throttling a world
but its eyes are dead weights,
if they drop inward
they drop clear through the universe

I can sense my words working their
way under its robe
though they struggle to remain free,
I sense a certain tugging in my head
as if roots were being pulled

at this moment I am barely a foot in height
my son's hand fills my chest
I speak but my son's mouth moves
I walk but my son's feet move
eventually he will slip the puppet over his body

Douglas Blazek

MY PAPER AXE

My mouth is broken
it has jagged edges that cut

in the center sits a dumb clot of words
it dries and flakes apart
falling on the backs of hands
dissolving like salt

do not approach my mouth
you will bleed till your body empties
and all fiber and bone collapse
no longer will you walk
with weight in your feet

I bite paper with my mouth
I carve an axe out of it
my paper axe
and you are holding it in your hands right now
and there is much land to clear
and a tall house to build

and a tremendous fire might be coming

CHARLES BUKOWSKI b. 1920

One of the most widely-known Polish-American poets, Charles Bukowski was born in Germany of a Polish-American father and a German mother. His family moved to Los Angeles when he was two years old. He writes: "I suppose my name is Polish, and all I know about the Poles is that they've lost a great many wars and there was some guy named Chopin who left Poland readily enough and hung around Paris."

He writes straightforward poetry that insists on the basic realities of working-class life, especially sex and drink. He distrusts abstractions and literary pretentions, especially a literary language dependent on English poetic traditions rather than immediate American realities. He has published many volumes of poetry, and his work is widely anthologized. His most recent book is *Burning in Water, Drowning in Flame* (Black Sparrow, 1974). He lives in Los Angeles.

Charles Bukowski

THE MEEK HAVE INHERITED

if I suffer at this
typewriter
think how I'd feel
among the lettuce-
pickers of Salinas?

I think of the men
I've known in
factories
with no way to
check out—
choking while living
choking while laughing
at Bob Hope or Lucille
Ball while
2 or 3 children beat
tennis balls against
the walls.

some suicides are never
recorded.

Charles Bukowski

THE LOSER

And the next time I remembered I'm on a table,
everybody's gone: the head of bravery
under light, scowling, flailing me down...
and then some toad stood there, smoking a cigar:
'Kid, you're no fighter,' he told me,
and I got up and knocked him over a chair;
it was like a scene in a movie, and
he stayed there on his big rump and said
over and over: 'Jesus, Jesus Whatsmatta wit
you?!' and I got up and dressed
(believe it or not)
the tape still on my hands and
wrote my first poem,
and I've been fighting
ever since.

SOMETHING

I'm out of matches.
the springs in my couch
are broken.
they stole my footlocker.
they stole my oil painting of
two pink eyes.
my car broke down.
eels climb my bathroom walls.
my love is broken.
but the stockmarket went up
today.

FRANK CEBULSKI b. 1938

Frank Cebulski's paternal grandfather was a raftsman on the Vistula before coming to America. The poet grew up in Colorado, where Polish was spoken in his home. "Unfortunately," he writes, "my younger sisters and I have lost our childhood ability to speak the language." He graduated from the University of Colorado in 1961, received an M.A. there two years later, and is currently finishing his doctorate in English at the University of California.

His poetry, in the tradition of Ezra Pound and T.S. Eliot, seems less intended for the average reader than for the cultural elite. Like Pound and Eliot, he takes western civilization for his theme, and like them he assumes much (often obscure) knowledge on the part of his readers. His books include *Corm* (Oyez, 1974) and *Mediterranean Sonnets* (forthcoming).

Frank Cebulski

XXXII

CARTHAGE

Not a poem (word) written since Carthage burned;
The fertile gift, all a bull's hide could spare,
Laid waste. Eidolons sweep the brine-burnt bare
Plain (wormbored reptilian furrows turned
Bellyward to the rotting sun) the earned
Expanse of an economic flair.
Hannibal dreams cities, peoples the air
With multitudes, labors undiscerned.
Elephants trumpet in terrific bright
Snow; their canopies, drivers, miniature
Toy palanquins, tumble. Two carriages race
Along the Po; horses, swords, steam in the light.
Machiavelli draws his sinister
Black cloak over a child's bloody face.

LXXIV

Yet, when I think
        of the psyche

as coiled

        as spun
in the double
helix of the

        DNA

with its crossrungs
        & magnificent
                laddered
            complexity

        the soul

    is not

        thereby

            belittled

LXXXVIII

ORPHEUS AND EURYDICE

That is a flower that strikes against wind
And sends the shadows of itself in deep
Darkness of hell where Eurydice fell
Back into Lethe's tapering blindness.

Vico veers where a spiral spins the mind;
Cyclic metempsychosis of death sleep
Animus approximates in gene gel,
Passing into each cell its ownkindness.

Orpheus! ORPHEUS! The black sands hiss.
The commandant lyre wrinkles in his hands.
His fear no box of history can play.

Grave Gabriel awakes the dead to this
Interlude of "thought-tormented music":
All things diminish by your start away.

Giovanni Battista Vico, an 18th century Italian philosopher, wrote of the "law of cycles" in the development of history.

VICTOR CONTOSKI b. 1936

Victor Contoski was born in Minneapolis, where he grew up in a Polish-American community. After graduating from the University of Minnesota, he lived in Poland from 1961 to 1964 teaching American literature, learning the Polish language, and marrying a native Pole. On his return to the United States, he entered graduate school at the University of Wisconsin, where he received a doctorate in American literature. His translations of contemporary Polish poets have appeared in a wide variety of magazines.

A Professor of English at Kansas University and an Associate Editor of *The Minnesota Review*, his most recent book is *Names* (New Rivers: St. Paul, 1979).

Victor Contoski

SALT

1

Salt spilled
on the wooden table.

Its crystals lie
like fallen snow.

Soon it will enter the wood
which will never bloom again.

2

The butcher sweats like a pig.
He covers himself with blood.
After work his clothes dry in the sun.

Salt turns them white.

He puts them back on and goes to the park
where he mounts a huge pedestal
thinking the people pay him homage.

But they are honoring salt.

3

A king's daughter
who worked for a witch
made salt with her tears.

She cried every day

till she filled a pail.

Put the tears of a princess
on your mashed potatoes.

4

Salt lies deep underground
like those we love.

Dirty men dig down
to stand amazed at its beauty.

They carve it into statues:
Christ at the Last Supper,
the Virgin Mary,
St. John of the Depths.

Then they leave their work
to the moisture of centuries.

But in the light of day
they can no longer worship
in high stone churches.

5

My first communion:

far down under the earth
someone placed on my tongue
a pinch of salt.

Victor Contoski

NIGHT ON THE PRAIRIE

for Harley Elliott

The pale hands of night
hold out her gift
a jewelled box.

She opens it
and dusk flows
from its well
like music

—the ebony violin
of Grazyna Bacewicz.

We enter
to find darkness
and more darkness.

Nothing to touch
so we fold our hands.

Nowhere to go
so we lie down.

Nothing to see
so we close our eyes

and see sparks

the new lamps lighting
light years away.

BILL (BOLES) COSTLEY

Bill Costley's mother was the middle daughter of Jan Kulik, a foreman on an estate in the village of Mosty Levyje near Grodno, now Soviet Lithuania. Her family sent her to Salem, Massachusetts to work as a housemaid in the homes of the wealthy Yankee gentry. His father was a Scot from Glasgow.

Of his relations with the Polish-American community Costley writes, "Dorothy Zuk hit me on the head with a gilded plaster eagle after milktime as we rummaged the toy-chest in Polish kindergarten; that ended the attendance, & has put me off on golden eagles since. What little Polish I learned thereafter was household use and all my prayers, from my mother. My father acquired some working Polish to converse with my grandparents who replaced his parents in his affections soon. He is buried in their family plot, the only non-Polish name on the headstone under Kulik. As he loved them, so did I, enough to adopt Boles Kulik as an altronym for poems on Polish subjects."

He works for the Institute of Human Relations in Boston and is a graduate student at Boston University.

Bill Costley

FOR DAD AND THE FACTORY
LYNN RIVER WORKS GE

it was ground into his oil-proof heels
with the chips off the lathe
& we smelled it
when he came in the door:
the Factory

it was transmitted through the floorboards
late in the night
& we heard it
in the sub-sonic test rumble:
the Factory

it was etched into my retinas
with the first poems I wrote
laying the oak-tree over it
as the three smokestacks blew:
the Factory

we lived by it with it & on it
everything but in it
& he spent most of his day there:
the Factory

tell me another advocate planning fable about it
tell me another corporate profit-sharing plan about it
tell me another post-war industrial lie about it

& let it eat you too.

it eats us.

Bill Costley

from KULIK / KRRULIK

I

    for Christmas, my half-Polish sister has given my son a bird
        whistle
    joined from a handful of unfinished pieces of Central European
        birch;
    I hold it in my hand; it holds my thinking
    of the neurological service of a Commonwealth hospital
    & its research floor:
    I cut out pieces of a lithographed Christmas shopping bag
    & tape them to the yellow tile wall, a Painted Bird of my
        designing;

II

Nearer easter, I learn from a patient, dislocated American branch
of the forests of Poland—
                my mother's name, Kulik,
is one of the brood of peasant names "taken from the birds."
            (hearing, years behind my back
            my mother's purling the sound
her family's name came from "krrulik, Kuulik, krrulik"
in the kitchen of my hand-painted grandmother's home . . .)

WILLIAM DORESKI

William Doreski grew up in a small town with a large Polish-American contingency, in which he found little sense of "community" as such. He sees music, poetry, and especially painting as the most important influences on his work. "It is important to me that Poland has an important, lively, accomplished group of writers working there right now: in a vague way I feel proud of them and sympathize with their difficulties. They influence my work through translations and through my ill-defined interest in them as political and social creatures, whose shoes I occassionally try to imagine myself in. But I am much closer to the American poets of my time, and even to American and English poets of the past, since we share the essential common bond of language."

He lives in Boston where he teaches at Goddard College. For several years he has operated a bookstore just off Harvard Square. His latest book is *The Testament of Isreal Potter* (Seven Woods: New York, 1976).

William Doreski

HANCOCK HILL IN MIDWINTER

The view is only a goad.
Downtown Boston rides the frost
to a deadend by the sea.
In Milton, houses tire of the dance.
If I jumped from here I'd touch
a hundred snowdrifts like eyelids
on the brow of the hill going down.
No phrenologist, still I'd know
what the earth thought of its latest
falling angel, guilty of faith.
The view tempts me toward anger
because I can't gather it up
like an armful of foxglove
and take it home for a still-life
that would fool me for an hour
or two while the flowers breathed;
fool me out of the suicide
of trying to catch the whole view
on the run. I'm unable to say
why I always consider such leaps
unlikely to be fatal, but
parallel to the flight of the sun.

SNOWSHOEING TO START THE NEW YEAR

New Year's Day: the moan of traffic
combines to translate sun and cold
and ruffles of snow
to spears of language in the mind:

one word, and painful,
swallowed like a sword for practice.

My snowshoes kick up storms
behind me, the prints are butterflies
with one shoulder hunched.
No one has preceded me in word or deed,
why should I turn my back to pray?

The lesson of that one vicious word
is that the dicta of Webster and Eliot
drip like runoff
beneath a crust that can hold me.

Never to see the low sun ripen,
never to stroke the sweating grass. . . .
A complex of bare deciduous branches
reminds me that like Aristotle
I have too many feelers out.

I could die freezing and pleased,——
on my back to memorize the map
of trees, its violent cities, fast highways.

Each step on snowshoes is a slap
of affection between lovers who've never met;
who can afford
to seem brutal while the sun's low.

Each step is one whole spoonful.
I'm inside the eye, it's so
blue here I should be swimming.

Two saplings fiddle in the wind
and invent my name.
The standards set by the last heavy snowstorm
condemn my career to an end
here, dwelling on sufficient fame.

William Doreski

ESTABROOK COUNTY

Bandages of rain, a narrow field.
Vees of geese flow north, faithful
to their one-track Canada route.
Three times I've trampled the same hill,
drunk all the fog from the view.

The reeking soil mints grass so green
it hurts my eyes as I strain
to touch the sky's erasures.
No one's home upstairs, I tell
the bluets crumpling in the breeze.

In this landscape a war was planned
and a botanist died shivering.
Here the ghost of a stallion
might thud from the woods, foaming,
to catch me on my knees for flowers.

The meekest species, shaped like bombs,
burst in terror by the road.
Viola triloba, *anemone*,
Trientalis——odors of compost
and flood mate around me, they grasp

my clothes with little pinchers,
they stalk me in rubber shoes.
I'm lost in seven hundred acres
of trails blazed clearly with blue.
No one notices how I hunch

past a ruined cabin, pockets
ripe with flowers; no one admits
anymore seeing what follows me—
furrowing the rich April mud,
poor vegetable, my green dragon tail.

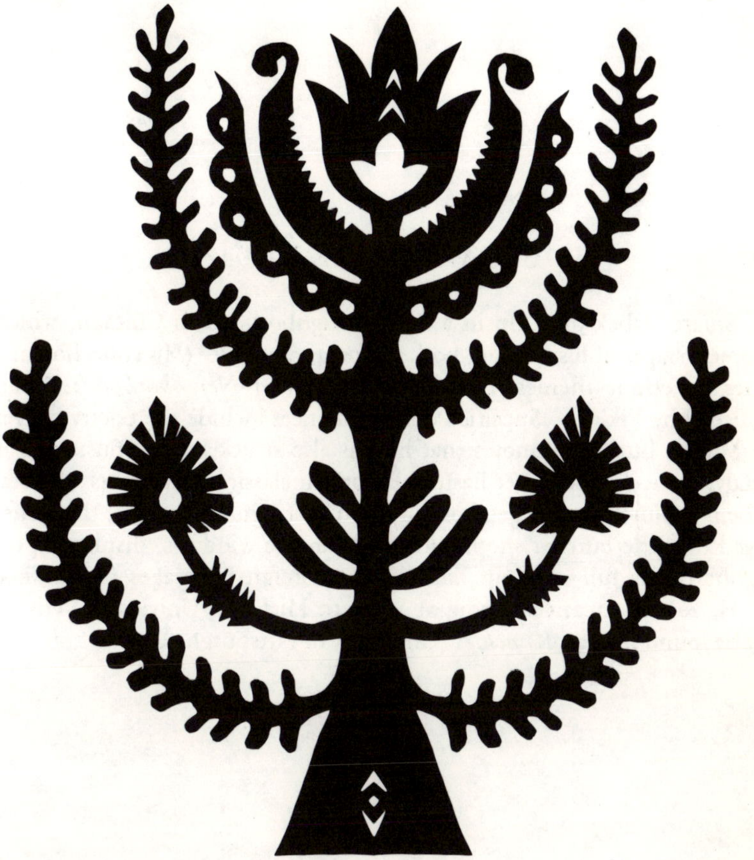

STUART DYBEK b. 1942

Stuart Dybek grew up in a Polish neighborhood in Chicago, which has become a staple of his writing, both fiction and poetry. (His collection of short stories on ethnic themes, *Childhood and Other Neighborhoods*, has been published by Viking). Specific Polish influences include the poetry of Herbert and Milosz, but Dybek notes that he was also struck by the music of Bartok, Kodaly, Janacek, and other Eastern European classical composers. "Listening to them conjured up images from my own past: grandmothers, the icons they prayed to, little butcher shops with ducks in the windows, displaced persons, neighborhoods full of them, and all the foreign languages of childhood."

He teaches creative writing at Western Michigan University. His poetry may be found in *Brass Knuckles* (University of Pittsburgh, 1979).

Stuart Dybek

VIVALDI

When I met Vivaldi it was dark,
a ragman lashed his horse's bells,
streets tilted into slow wind tunnels,

no, it was another night, in winter,
snow as soft as opium, two winoes wassailed
down an alley through a milk truck's ruts,

in the subways a violin was whistling
down chrome tracks, past cobalt semaphores,
rats and pennies underneath the 3rd rail . . .

Has it ever been so quiet that you've heard
the manhole covers rumble when the El goes overhead?
Icicles growing? Could you tell the difference
between the sound of filaments in the light bulbs
burning down, and a dulcimer played in a padded cell?

A meager music hovers everywhere:
at mouths of drains, echoing stairwells
where girls in muslin disappear
whispering "allegro."

When I closed my eyes,
less than a ghost,
Vivaldi cupped a mouth harp
like a match against the wind.

Stuart Dybek

PENANCE

It was always Good Friday
those Saturday afternoons.
Stooped babkas in black coats
and babushkas, kneeling
in marble aisles
before racks of vigil candles,
faces buried in hands.
Weeping echoes through the dim church
as foreign as their droned
language of prayer.
I stood in line
waiting the priest's question,
"Alone or with others?"
and my turn in Confession,
trying to imagine
the terrible sins of old women.

Stuart Dybek

THE KNIFE-SHARPENER'S DAUGHTER

A drain spout splashing
rusty stains on concrete,

the taste of doorknobs
you kiss before squinting

through the musty keyhole
at the knife-sharpener's daughter

while across the city
the knife-sharpener

limps his pushcart
with its dinging axles,

with its screeching whetstone
up wet alleys

crying: scissors! knives! axes!

DONALD FINKEL

Born in New York City and raised by his Russian mother and maternal grandmother, until recently Donald Finkel did not think of himself as Polish, though his father's parents emigrated from Poland. Only after repeated requests from Poles to translate his work, did he become interested in Polish culture. "The first volume I located was Milosz's incredible anthology, *Post-War Polish Poetry*, and I was enchanted to discover what a treasury had been waiting for me all those years—the work of poets like Miłosz, Różewicz, Herbert, Harasymowicz, etc. Since then I've read what I could find in English, but what has especially compelled me is the poetry of Zbigniew Herbert, with whom I felt an instant sympathy. If I didn't know better, I'd conclude that his poetry exerted a continuous mysterious influence over mine from the very beginning, in regard to both tone and subject matter. It wouldn't be surprising, of course, if that influence has become more pronounced in the past half dozen years."

He has an M.F.A. from the University of Iowa and teaches at Washington University in St. Louis. His poetry has been widely anthologized and translated. His newest book, *The Detachable Man*, is forthcoming from Atheneum.

Donald Finkel

WEEDS

I have no quarrel with bindweed
when I was a boy
dandelion was king of the gypsies
grinning in the park
through his sooty teeth

nettle and milkweed
burdock, chicory

the weeds move in
an army of poor relatives
shouldering the gladioli

boneset, heal-all
meadowsweet, mother of aspirin

and the weeds move out
impudent garlic the Greeks
called Stinking Rose
chewed against drunkness
head colds strangers worms the plague
misses her shiftless cousins

goat's-bears, sow-thistle
daisy and mullen

she sidles to the roadside
and sticks out her thumb

all through the winter goldfinch dines
at thistle's table

Donald Finkel

WHAT MY HEAD IS FOR

To keep my ears from squabbling
to pound on the door of judgment
when my knuckles are sore

to keep my nose out of the sewer
to hold souvenirs, old keys
worn yellow pebbles, a parching tongue
cracked like a castoff shoe

to lift my eyes above my appetite
to read the writing over urinals
peek through windows, make out scrawls
in matchbooks praising black motels
I never slept in, bearing
one last match, whose rosy head
I still may strike against the dark

a head with a future, not like this one
doomed never to flower on my shoulders
destined ever to nod nod on its stalk
at the merest breath of reason

a head that does not settle
in the cup of my palms like cloudy water
a head I might strike
on the smog-brown backside of night
and set the blue tongues singing under my soup

Donald Finkel

HOW THINGS FALL

Shoes fall on their feet
angels fall to their knees
the note falls due
the words fall short
the butterfly falls to a blade of grass
and clings, still flittering

dust settles, stars decline
curtains plunge and splendor sprawls
the day falls into place
the sleeper falls back on his dream
princes fall out and troops fall in

a pound of feathers falls like a pound of flesh
the balances pitch and tremble
leaves fall like lovers, suicides like snow
drifting reluctantly plummeting eagerly
whispering in the wind they make

when the temple falls
every shard becomes a temple
when the city crumples
won't the masons have their day
a feast of heavenly mortar
an orgy of stones

JOHN GOGOL

John Gogol grew up in the Polish-American community of Westfield, Massachusetts. He belonged to the Polish National Catholic Church which held the entire service in Polish. As a teenager he read the Polish Romantic poets, particularly Slowacki and Mickiewicz, who became the first major literary influences on his work. His first published poem was titled "The Red and the White."

After receiving a B.A. in European History from Clark University, he moved west for his further education, an M.A. in German from the University of Washington and his own independent studies of the American Indian. Currently he is a Ph.D. candidate in Comparative Literature. He lives in Portland Oregon, where he edits *American Indian Basketry* and co-edits the literary magazine *Mr. Cogito*. His poetry is available in *Native American Words* (Tahmahnawis: Portland, Oregon, 1973). He has published translations of contemporary German, Russian, and Polish poetry.

John Gogol

NATIVE AMERICAN DESERT

The rimrock runs red,
bleeds ochre
through porous bones.
Obsidian litter
flashes beyond blackness,
fills the emptiness
of ancient camps.
The inhabitants are gone,
rounded up, corralled,
branded English, or
tongues cut out,
now forgotten.
Those that live here still
hide under stones,
among the petroglyphs,
protected by guardian lizard,
appointed in stone,
and in flesh.

Killdeer cries
echo anguish
among dried bones
of broken men.
Birds still live well here,
but how long
till only
their bones remain?

John Gogol

NATIVE AMERICAN WORDS

Obsidian points race the last wash of the waves,
then rest, tentative,
form a trail in time and space,
remember the tensed second of youth,
the unleashing
to part the reeds
or plough the waves,
cold sharpness on a quest
for the warmth of a feathered nest.
Then, strength spent,
they hibernated,
holding onto words
heard in the wind.

Black barbed bullets,
jeweled luck,
tell us a tale, tell us of time,
tell and retell,
batter the barriers at our ears
which hear ever less.

Lulled into sleep
by secure sounds, and image,
we no longer hear into silence;
too firmly grasping the lines,
present, past, and future,
we hold onto comfort,
tree as door, and stone as step,
too numb to follow the sharpness
into native words.

John Gogol

UNTITLED

God spoke to us in Polish
>spoke purple silk banners
>only partially comprehended,
>divine words intuitively understood,
>drawn into the nostrils
>from burning candles and incense,
>through flowers, and grandmothers.
>
>English, language of schoolbooks,
>What god would speak such a boring language?

TERRY KENNEDY b. 1941

Terry Kennedy remembers that when she was growing up in Bellows Falls, Vermont, her friends went on picnics or saw the Ice Follies, while she helped her babcia do the washing and ironing for the priests at the Polish Catholic Church. "Sometimes while she scrubbed their shirts up and down on an old, tin washboard she would take to weeping and wailing about her mother and father and other relatives left behind in Poland while at 16 she set sail for the great, American dream."

Kennedy graduated from Regis, a Catholic college, the first woman in her family to earn a degree. Beset by physical and emotional problems, she says she writes to escape her fears. "My work is still pre-occupied with themes of lost childhood and survival. I guess I write not so much because of my Polish blood but rather because the way I see it—if I don't write I am doomed!" A mother of three, she lives in Duxbury, Massachusetts, and works as a free-lance journalist and investigative reporter. Her poetry is available in *Durango* (The Smith, 1979).

Terry Kennedy

THE PILLOW

mornings i am so cocky
talking of dreams as if they were movies
i joke about the beating wings of my father
or the quicksilver eyes of a lover

i shove my pillow under the sheets
and cover my mother's haunting grin

but nights i shake like a gambler
losing the jackpot
in the raining blood room
where everything counts
or the formaldehyde room
with the drain in the floor

so i press my face into the pillow
into the tomatoey scent of my skin
i wrap my arms around
that foam rubber thing

i hold on as if it were god

Terry Kennedy

THERE IS NO METAPHOR FOR HATE

my husband with his fast car
and his fast pace
and his fast job
i hate the way he rushes
to keep up with his importance
the whole world is waiting for him to arrive
every morning when he is late getting up
it is because he is under so much pressure
he needs a little more sleep
everytime he goes off with the boys
it is because he is under so much pressure
he needs time to relax
everytime he does anything rude or forgets things
it is because he is under so much pressure
he can't be patient or has something
really important on his mind
one day i realized i hated him
because he was under so much pressure
and i was under him

HOLDING ON

each time i think about leaving him
i am sure i am right
i ought to go
my bones ache to be rid of his tonnage
soon i will be too old for his tastes
too wrinkled in the face and belly
he will see to it that i am ugly
i stay for too many of the wrong reasons
too many of the reasons we've all come to
believe are good
i see the frightened eyes of my children
they are tangibles
holding me here
cemented to needs
it is the cool green touch of money that i want
something to put my fists around

LEONARD KRESS b. 1950

Leonard Kress speaks Polish, "but not fluently." His family came to the United States in the late nineteenth century from Wilno and Warsaw. Polish and Polish-American cultural traditions are, he writes, not only important but "form a basis for my work."

He was born in Toledo, grew up in Philadelphia, and graduated from Temple University with a B.A. in religion and the University of Illinois at Chicago with an M.A. in English. His book of short stories about life in Polonia, *A Stork Built a Nest by the House of the Priest*, is currently looking for a publisher, as are his translations of Kazimiera Iłłakowiczówna. He has published one book of poetry, *Tryst: From the Life and Death of Chopin* (Lalka, 1976).

Leonard Kress

BOBOWA

1

They say the Tarters sharpened their swords
on the cornerstone of the gray church
and point to the ground-out indentation
in the granite. The bones of the church
they say are held together by the whites
of eggs and the bell so stiff it lurch-
es on thursday only. A huge lamb like a pagan
Zeus grazes on the altar and from
the hillside a shallow river slits
the throat of a the treebearded hills.
A horse with the childish determination
of an ikon trods the night minyon road.

They say the Jews burned down the town
not meaning to of course, but stuffed
in their scroll-lean quarter at prayer
or god knows what by flames
the town like a bush was ravished.

2

      In the rain the roof
      of the thatched farm
      falls in clumps over
      the blue wash wall

      Who is it calling to us
      in the bleating throat
      of the lamb tethered to a fence . . .

Someone known . . .
Someone abandoned . . .
The town itself
in the yoke of the hill's memory.

And they still weave here:

    day through night   light crossing morn
              night over dawn
Young girls slam the heavy looms
and mothers lace the town
like a white bridal gown.

One sings in the night
by the glowing railroad tracks:

"the wind through the hazelwood rustled
how quick the leaves turn green
the girl stood alone weeping
how quick was the boy to leave."

Leonard Kress

THE COMING OF DARKNESS IN ISTEBNA

at dusk
a tree which the afternoon had knitted
into an old woman
stands bent over a hoe

the sound of wax churchbells drip
in the distant hills
which are only shadows
of the mountainous sky

the old woman bent over a hoe
grows stiff as a haystack
and sinking like a stricken cow
bows to the expectant earth.

                        Beskid Ślask, Poland

Leonard Kress

ON THE BUS TO ZAKOPANE

I want to place my hands
on the brown glistening head
of the rucksacked peasant woman
sitting in front of me

I want to remove her faded kerchief
slow and deliberate like the stiff
blouse of a virgin
and unbraid the coil of her hair
releasing snakes from their prison of soil

I want her to throw down
the burdens of the marketplace
and together we will listen
to the sound of eggs
crack against the side of a passing hut

I will buy her new golden earrings
that shine like the points of her mistrusting eyes
and skirts more flowerful
than mountain pastures in May

She is old enough to be my mother
and I want her to sing to me

I want to lie beside her
in a new threshed field
hidden from my own desperate life
by an endless row of haystacks

KARL KULIKOWSKI b. 1920

Karl Kulikowski sees no special Polish literary influences on his work. His Polish-American upbringing, however, was instrumental in forming the values by which he lives: "the work ethic, respect for the elderly, a religious feeling (which I questioned and explored for a good many years, probably more than many other writers, and returned to the religion of my forebears) and a Polish thick-headedness that does not know how to quit—which makes the Polish people a difficult people for subjugation."

He lives in the Bronx, where he edits two literary magazines, *Gusto* and *Driftwood East*. His most recent book is *Haiku, Senryu, and Poetry* (Gusto, 1978).

Karl Kulikowski

MUSIC IN GREENPOINT

Reading Yevtushenko and the wedding
Carried me back to Greenpoint in the Twenties.
The Grudzinskis visiting us on a Saturday night.
Pan Grudzinski taking out his accordion.
He had bought a new one.
One he displayed proudly—
Unlike the old one that he had to pump with his feet.
The Grudzinskis were musical.
Felix, the eldest, played the violin very well,
Also his brother Eddie's piano, and his father's accordion.
Eddie, the youngest, played the piano fairly well and also
       his father's accordion.
Panie Grudzinska and my mother were childhood friends
       from Poland.
Although' it was Prohibition, my father had whiskey and beer.
My mother put out food, although it was the Depression.
No matter how poor we were,
When anyone visited
Morning, noon, or night
My parents put out Zakunski.
Pan Grudzinski played well.
All old Polish favorites.
Sometimes Pan Mayewski would be there with his violing
       somewhat squeaky.
The music traveled in the air.
The air is world-wide.
How far did it travel?

They are all long-gone now.
Only my mother who had it hardest
Still holds on.
(Our mother in blue appeared to her one night

many years ago,
when she was depressed and crying,
and said,
"Manya, do not cry.
You will live to be eighty-five.")
Sometime ago we saw many old names when
    we visited St. Charles Cemetery on the Island,
Paying respects to my brother-in-law, Ben,
    and my father.
His name was Marion. They called him Mike.
Names familiar from Greenpoint.
There were so many familiar names.
It seemed that all Greenpoint had moved into the
    cemeteries, buried far in the suburbs.

No room in cemeteries closer to the city.

The music?
What happened to the music?
Is it still there?
Can one hear?
There are some few who can still hear.

STEPHEN LEWANDOWSKI b. 1947

In 1910 Stephen Lewandowski's paternal grandparents moved from a small village outside Poznań to Chicago. There his grandfather worked in the mills and factories, while his grandmother cured sausage behind the stove and raised seven children. His father, who speaks Polish, was born and raised in Chicago but moved to Buffalo in 1929. The poet, who does not, was born and raised in upstate New York, studying literature, philosophy, and folklore at Hamilton College, Pendle Hill, Washington University, and Cooperstown. His latest book is *Inside & Out* (Crossing, 1979).

He writes that his crucial concerns include: "cutting and splitting enough wood to keep warm this winter, playing softball every summer, gardening for fresh use and canning, cooking, reading and writing. Nothing fancy."

Stephen Lewandowski

WIND BEFORE DAWN

Flapping at four o'clock
What can rattle rattles.
The wind throws itself around
like a willful child. It's easy
to attribute emotions to the elements
on such nights. Bits & pieces of
light things fly through the air.
The weeping willow looming
over my neighbor's house whips
itself furiously, animated by
thousands of airy penitentes.
Gusts batter against dark windows
of the sleeping town; here & there
a limb crashes down, shingles tear off.
Not much to show for such an effort—
"and I'll huff and I'll puff"—
what a time to be visited by wolves.
My old house stirs itself, creaky
joints & joists, stone & brick grinding
& me in my bed then dreaming of sails
& flying through the air, now sitting &
drinking tea in the face of a big wind.

Stephen Lewandowski

WILLOWS

asleep in this shade
the horses of my dreams
have it their way;
they gallop to you.

HERON

rising from dreams
wing beats match
the strokes of my heart
carry me over the lake

Stephen Lewandowski

ANTON & ANNA LEWANDOWSKI

Grandfather handled steel as
roller-man in the Tonawanda mills.
Introduced my father to the men on his shift
"This is my youngest son Stanley"
& gave him a quarter to bring a pail
of beer from the corner tavern
to wash down their tin box lunches.
I only remember him
as a slight man in skivvies,
rumors of his long dying &
my father coming back to the car—
face gone pale, blue eyes set.
But memory can only affirm the past
& I want no such affirmation.
I know my life flows.
I can no more bring you to life again
than I could calm my fear of your wife,
Anna my grandmother, who spoke Polish
too loud, too quick, would grab at me.
She was crying; she wanted to hold
her grand-child to her breast.
Blood of her blood. Blood of my blood.
What caused that shrinking?
I was raised in another place,
another time, among cold people.
Coolness haunts me grandmother. Cure me.
Hold me. When was the last time I saw you?
Blood whispers through my dreams.
It has a life of its own, which I ask
my share of. Speak to me, my heart.
I'll understand where the words come from.

JOSEPH LISOWSKI b. 1944

Joseph Lisowski grew up in an ethnic neighborhood in Pittsburgh, where he lived with his younger brothers and sisters, his maternal grandparents, an uncle, an aunt, and his parents—all under one roof. "My first language was Polish," he writes, "and when I started school the language of primary instruction was Polish. When I was in second grade, the state intervened and English became the rule." He regrets losing the language.

His education includes a degree in accounting and an M.A. in English from Duquesne University, and a doctorate in English from the State University of New York at Binghamton. At present he is Associate Professor at J. Sargeant Reynolds Community College in Richmond, Virginia.

Joseph Lisowski

FAMILY TIES

I looked in the mirror long enough
To see my childhood still sucking the dug
Of my mother and noticed how her blue eyes
Lulled me to sleep with a song of grandfather
And father and grandmother and all the children after.

I was stunned at first then curious.
But when I decided to turn away I saw
Myself suck harder and felt the cord draw tighter
Until it seemed that I was gathered again in her belly
And heard nothing but the echoes of family funeral cries.

FOR YEARS

The nights rolled in like a tremble of flesh.
They felt like waves of an earthquake.
I curled on my bed listening for a voice,
Something to remove the pressure—my heart—
My head heavy with the weight of families
And falling.

Joseph Lisowski

ON THE WAY HOME

The moon is full of ice
And the dogs are cold and howling
Under the streetlights—
Sycamores hang over the cemetery fence.
The headstones are pale
As frozen mother's milk.
I think of snow, my new baby,
And my grandfather's white, white hands.

JOHN MINCZESKI b. 1947

John Minczeski's grandfather left Jelenia Góra as a young man and came to America knowing no English. He settled in the Polish community in South Bend, where he sold insurance. "Other than influences from Zbigniew Herbert, Tadeusz Różewicz, and Jerzy Harasymowicz," Minczeski writes, "I think the Polish influence has been fairly neglegible, with the exception that I have some more things in draft on my grandfather and great-grandfather. I think I'm turning more of my attention to Poland now, and would like to visit Poland sometime."

He lives in St. Paul, where he works as a typesetter and editorial assistant for New Rivers press. *The Spiders* (New Rivers, 1979) is his first book of poetry.

John Minczeski

OUR LADY OF WHEAT

If somehow the wheat in the vase
were a princess
imprisoned in wheat.

If I had a bundle of wheat in my heart

I could say "Princess, be free!
Step out of the wheat."

I could take you far away
from the charms of your stepmother.

But you are only wheat.
You are sown,
the wind is lovely,
you think you are going to die,
then you die.

My princess, I will keep you in the wheat.
Stay there.
I will love you no less.

John Minczeski

THE MAN WITH THE WOODEN HEART

My heart is wood.
Fist shaped
fist sized.

Worn smooth
by water.

Every friday
an old woman
dusts it inside
and out.

Every year
someone
burns it.

Sometimes
it smolders
for months
like an old stump.

Every year
my heart is smaller.

It is growing into
a child's heart.

Jesus said
unless you become
as little children

on one hand
I am waiting to enter the kingdom

on the other
I am waiting
to wash ashore.

A MAN IS FOLLOWING HIS HEART

A man is following his heart
through a swamp.
He holds a string
so he won't get lost.
His heart
the fairest thing in the world
he would follow anywhere.

Now it is reading to him
fairy tales so frightening
he covers himself with a white
          cloth.
The heart likes it
and turns into a woman.

I want to see you naked, she says.
He takes off his clothes.
I want to see you without your skin.
He removes his skin.

She pushes the muscles aside
crawls into the place where
the heart belongs.

Now the man has a woman
for a heart.

ED OCHESTER b. 1939

Ed Ochester's grandfather, William Olchevski, came to this country from Poland sometime during the last part of the 19th century and settled in Brooklyn. He had four sons, anglicized his name, and when his oldest boy was in his teens, left the family forever. "My grandmother and the boys quite systematically (it appears) destroyed practically all records of him."

Only in his twenties did Ochester become exposed to Polish culture: Jan Kott's criticism of Shakespeare, the poems of Zbigniew Herbert, and Victor Contoski's *Four Contemporary Polish Poets*. Of his own work he writes: "I want a poetry immensely moving in immediate, human terms—the theme is 'love one another or die,' though the authority for it isn't Christian—but a poetry that doesn't trade in the random eccentricities of the merely personal."

He teaches at the University of Pittsburgh, where he also edits the Pittsburgh Poetry Series. His latest book is *The End of the Ice Age* (Slow Loris, 1977).

Ed Ochester

AS YOU LEAVE

In the old country
of the heart
people whistled
alone in the woods
all night.

They trundled milk
from black barns
as the cattle
walked away from them
for years.

Grandchildren they never saw
read their sour letters
from the cigarmaker's shops:

you will live
beneath the shadow
for ever and ever
and ever.

Ed Ochester

THE TOWER AT THE END OF THE WORLD

We let down our hair
so that our sisters and brothers
may climb up.
We hold their faces in our hands,
cupping the flesh in our palms
for hours.
In the dim hall our bodies
pulse and grow
like babies.
It is warm as blood
as we dance carefully, cross-step,
the long line of us
up the circular ramp.
Our lips fuse
into smooth muzzles.
How soft our eyes have become,
like the beloved children of giants.
At the top we lean over the parapet
in the small rain.
The black woods are empty.
Far below a few handfuls of white flowers
travel with us
slowly as the stars.

Ed Ochester

IN THE LIBRARY

the silent girl,
the ugly one,
waits out the spring above her books;
her thoughts poise between
pleasures in the strong sun
and the despair her fragile body brings.

She is the white crane
staring downward,
conscious of her reed neck
that the smallest stone can break.

MARK PAWLAK B. 1948

Mark Pawlak, a second-generation Polish-American, grew up in the Polish community in Buffalo, New York. "Within my extended family there was little awareness of the 'high culture' of the 'Old Country'—I discovered Chopin on my own through a mail-order record company—for the daily concern was keeping food on the table and a roof overhead. However, Polish domestic customs were more or less preserved in my home and when the clan gathered, and then most memorably at Christmas time and Easter when a grandmother laid her tables with dishes of Kiełbasa and pierogi, with czarnina and barszcz, placek, chrusciki. . . . " The tales told at these gatherings "have profoundly influenced the development of, the imagery, emotional fabric, and diction of my poetry."

He lives in Somerville, Massachusetts. He works as Academic Coordinator and Co-Director of The Group School, an alternative high school for poor and working class youth in Cambridge. His latest book is *The Buffalo Sequence* (Copper Canyon, 1977).

Mark Pawlak

from THE BUFFALO SEQUENCE

xi

" . . . can't you hear the whistle blowing?
rise up so early in the morn."

    died: the grandfathers.
and buried with them
are the tunes they sang when we were little.
the muscular waists of grandfathers
continue, in our memories,
to toil up the day's last steep avenue.

—we should now stand up and pledge allegiance to the flag
of this country
where everyone makes a lot of money and gets ahead.

    died: the grandmothers.
who have passed on their recipes of duck's blood and love
to daughters and granddaughters.
their ethnic apron strings are desperate tentacles
too short to hold all the children
and yet they never let us go.

—now we should all pick up our clumsy 3rd grade pencils
and write the letter A perfectly, with no accent.

    died: joe what's-his-name-ski,
the foreman who lived down the block.
according to the obituary, he suffered for years
of dreaming he was a time card,
that night after night,
was swallowed in its own pool of sweat.

—now we should take a lesson from Carnegie,
and save pennies in our piggy banks
which are round and hollow like the hours.
so when we retire, we can collect,
each day, for eternity, sixty crackled knucklebones.

but, for the time being, we've learned enough
of newspapers and obituaries.

     we should all remember to return single file, after lunch,
and then apply ourselves really hard. —who knows?
when grown up, one of us may write a book
about the bloated livers which inhabit our streets;
or that speaks of parenthood as a white rib
from which drop jewels of amber beer,
that fall inward and inward, mingling with suspicions.

     we should apply ourselves,
and the smartest may even get a scholarship to college;
and become a professional something-or-other. —god knows!
would we then have to live in
these tubercular houses,
which shoulder to shoulder, wheeze and lean,
which lean so on the intimacies of window panes?

now we should go over the homework.
there are a few stories, but for grammar and spelling,
would have gotten A's.

     in Jim's story, he talks of the nights:
—Quiet down, it's late! they growl.
and shadows behind the corner delicatessen whisper:
—what are pennies but dirty coppers?
he says that somehow, Saturdays, glazed with erotic sweat
bears another child, another perfect tear,
from which the jaundiced moon cannot get free.
               —but that's life eh?

    Judy tells: behind drawn curtains,
you can count on there being
three despairing coffee cups
who are speaking of the children and ageing and
—it's your deal, while playing cards at the kitchen table.
she is troubled by the saliva of their sisterly jealousies,
how all the while it erodes a gutter
through the 1 heart of young cousins
that never thinks it will be 2.

    the last story is Bill's.
his theme is a summer visit
to relatives in Buffalo, Cleveland and Chicago.
he remembers how, evenings, those cities
relaxed the yellowing skin of their geographies;
which makes him think how this city is like any other
where we are born,
according to the file cards and certificates,
very small, —and for what?

    but now it is 3 o'clock. 3 o'clock.
3 o'clock in our experience.
we should take a moment to recall
how we haven't lived up to what's expected of us.
and remember, on the way home, to stop in the church
black as widow cloth inside, to make confession.

PHIL PAWLOWSKI b. 1948

Phil Pawlowski was educated at the State University of New York at Buffalo, where he received a B.A. in music. A native of Buffalo, he worked at the Behelehem Steel Coke Ovens, the subject of his first successful poems. Then he turned to his background. "Since I live in a Polish neighborhood and was raised by Polish-American parents, the Polish-American experience via second and third generation is a way of life for me. Writing about it was practically inevitable." His Polish vocabulary is limited to a few phrases.

A strong influence on his work has been the poetry of his friend Mark Pawlak, who made him aware of the possibilities of writing from a hometown perspective. "Incidentally," he adds, "I don't have a Polish accent (so I'm told) unless I become very excited."

Phil Pawlowski

WALTZ IN "A" MINOR

Sunday in the parlor.
The over-stuffed furniture.
She commands her son:
"Play me some Chopin."
He responds in "A" minor.
The sad waltz and a chalice
of Polish earth appear.
Chopin in a French Salon.
Mother and son in a Buffalo parlor.
And melody in the bass.

Time dissolves in three beats to the measure.
Majorca sunshine in East Side Sleet.
Perfume of the Motherland
Rising from a spinet.
Blonde wood
              Dark hair
                          White fingers

Swaying in time to the past.
Swaying in time to the past.

Phil Pawlowski

LANGUAGE LESSON

I

"Living room" is "parlor."
Front window is "okno."
In "okno" is "lampa."
"Ale fajna lampa!"

II

At the door we bless each other.
"Zostajcie z bogiem."
(May God be with you).
"Idź z bogiem."
(May God go with you).

III

On the street we greet a friend.
"Jak sie masz?"
(How's it going)?
"Dobrze."
(Good).

IV

We hurry to church.
The bells are ringing.
Such a fine sound!
Now,
    In what language do the bells ring!

Phil Pawlowski

KLUSKI (NOODLES)

The dough is kneaded.
Flour dust is fairy dust.
Now the rolling pin.
Newton's laws of motion.

The knife is sharp.
Scraping sounds on the bread board.
The dough of indifference pierced.
MOTHER MAKES KLUSKI.
MOTHER MAKES KLUSKI.

That old recipe for those noodles
Transmitted in blood and milk
From some distant plain:
      Give me a chicken.
      Give me wheat.
      Give me love.

JOHN PIJEWSKI b. 1952

John Pijewski attended a Polish grammar school in Boston, Our Lady of Częstochowa, taught by Felician nuns. His parents, who have been in the United States twenty nine years, speak only Polish. He also speaks the language, "though not with a large vocabulary." He has no connection with the Polish community in Boston, "though my parents belong to a Polish parish and shop in the handful of Polish stores open in the city; whatever I know about the community is second-hand and often colored by my mother's rather charming misconceptions."

He graduated from Boston University and received an M.A. from the University of New Hampshire. Currently he teaches at Boston University. His first collection of poetry, *Sunday Dinner with Uncle Jozef*, is searching for a publisher, and he is working on translations of various contemporary Polish poets.

John Pijewski

BURYING MY FATHER

Before they lowered him into the grave
I climbed inside his coffin.

In darkness I held his cold hand,
Sang Polish nursery rhymes,
Told fables, recited the alphabet.
When my voice gave way

I dug myself out
And saw old fruit dancing in orchards,
Violins strolling through a park,
Hats grazing on sunny pastures.

All my brothers and sisters
Stood like trees in a field. Their arms
Held birds that sang a certain music
So distinctly that I knew

If I had ever paused to listen
I would have heard it all my life.

John Pijewski

MY BROTHER'S DEAF DAUGHTER

(for A.H.)

Walking on the beach I caught myself
Talking to her. I had forgotten
She could not hear me, in the same way
I could not hear what the waves,
Stuttering on the beach, were telling me.

We banked ourselves atop a sand dune
And I tried to make sense of that
Monotonous sound. A bee droned by and I
Started, but Ann, unafraid, watched it
Float soundlessly across the sky.

We waded through water, stood still
Long enough to spot a striped bass
Swim past our feet. Did the motions
Of its slow fins say something to Ann
That I could never hear?

All day I longed to place my ear
Next to the conch of her ear
And listen for that distant ocean,
That beach abandoned inside her skull,
The water, sand dunes, endless blue sky.

On our way home we stopped by
A row of sunflowers. Ann, her arms
Upraised, ran around those giant flowers
While their yellow petals cupped
Toward the sun, listened to sunlight.

John Pijewski

NIGHT WALK

In the cold clarity of autumn night
Under a cold moon
I knew the bird was long dead,
Husked of feathers—rasped rat hairs
Stuck in gray wood.
Bones snapped when stepped on.
Its empty black eyesockets stared me down,
Turned me back.
The cold moon bright behind me.
My shadow led me home.

Just like that darkness entered each door,
Entered each window.
The black sky stepped into my bedroom.
Tiny stars pinholed through this sky blinked
Eyedrops of light.
I could not sleep until I
Stepped back into the night,
With my thumb smudged the moon out,
Tucked the sky beneath my chin.
Goodnight.

JOHN CALVIN REZMERSKI b. 1942

"We never listened to Chopin or read Mickiewicz when I was a kid," Rezmerski writes. "We listened to polkas and jokes and hunting stories at the St. Joseph Society's 'Polish Hall', and we called each other 'Polack' and were glad when people spelled our names right without comment. Any influence of Poland in my work has been filtered through this experience of being a third-generation member of a small Polish-American working-class community in the Allegheny Mountains, sharing a town with similar communities of other hyphenated Americans, mostly Italian. My father's father (born in Poland) often spoke Polish with my grandmother (first in her family born in America), and with their relatives and neighbors. I remember being badly intimidated by my great-grandmother, a tiny farm woman who frightened me not because she spoke Polish, but because she spoke no English that was intelligible to me. She seemed somehow supernatural."

A native of Pennsylvania, he was educated at Gannon College, John Carroll University, and the University of Kansas. He teaches English at Gustavus Adolphus College in Minnesota. His book *Held for Questioning* (University of Missouri, 1969) won the Devins Memorial Award for poetry. His latest book is *An American Gallery* (Three Rivers, 1977).

John Calvin Rezmerski

GRANDFATHER

At your anniversary Mass in July
the holy water was polluted
and nobody noticed.
Fewer of your friends came out this spring,
and Grandma wilts a little each summer
with the beans and the tomatoes.
The garden is played out,
even the worms don't go there so much.
The only thing that has stayed the same
is the smell of the sulfite smoke
and it no longer smells like money.
There is a stairway to your porch now,
and a hold between dining room and kitchen
to pass cups and dishes through.
I bet there is an old quart of peach brandy
in the cellar, and a tobacco can
hidden with some emergency money forgotten
while you waited in bed for your heart to quit.
It is your voice I remember best,
still half Polish,
and the roughness of your faded black sweater.
Remembering your whiskers on my cheeks
makes me feel like I'm six again.
The family never gets together
to play Pinochle any more.
The chicken house is empty,
even the dogs are gone
that stayed there when the last chicken was eaten.
It seems to me you used to keep pigeons.
Grandpa, if you had known my God
he would have protected you from yours.
He would have.

Your children are prospering
and you have dozens of great grandchildren.
Since you died we have acquired new one-way streets
and another stoplight.
And they're finally going to pave your street.
And according to the papers
Poland is still there.

John Calvin Rezmerski

SECOND MARRIAGE

He divorced his wife
and married whiskey,
and forgot how to fight.
He spoke less than before,
"How are you, neighbor?"
barely remembering the names
of old friends.

After his wife left,
he began to take long walks,
some of which he came back from.
Strange little bruises
appeared on his face,
and cuts on his fingers,
and he limped as if
kicked in the shins.

Whiskey was beating him up,
unfaithful whiskey
who had whispered
such words of love,
didn't understand him.

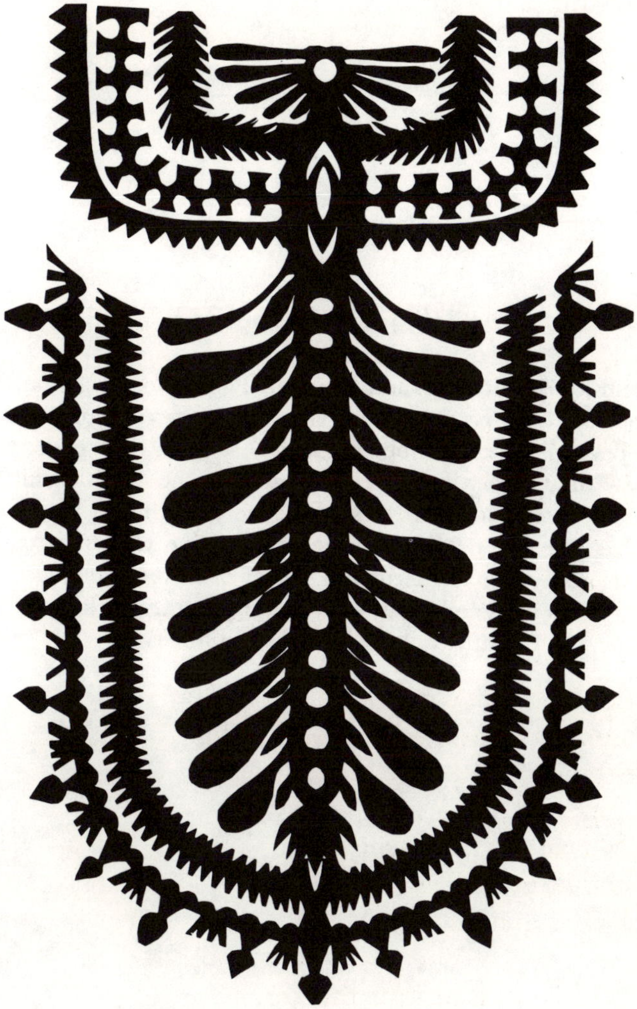

MARTIN J. ROSENBLUM b. 1946

Martin Rosenblum's grandmother left Poland for Appleton, Wisconsin, just before the Nazi occupation. "Grandma's stucco house on Mary Street was just beyond the ridge from my house, so I'd sit at her long, oak table on the way to and from home, eating hamentaschen and listening to family history as she would crochet." He speaks no Polish but is fluent in Hebrew.

He has received a Ph.D. in English from the University of Wisconsin-Milwaukee, and works as Executive Director of Lawyers for the Creative Arts in Chicago. His most ambitious work, a long poem, *The Werewolf Sequence* (Membrane, 1974) is still available from the publisher.

Martin J. Rosenblum

can't get back
to sleep trapped
even breath/my footsteps
on stairs
in freezing morning they
        echo like our cat
        licking its belly
at the foot of the bed
at sunrise i open
a jar of milk & am feeling
            nite thru
            window shade
the hall lite divides on my hands
over your very round stomach with
our baby kicking inside as we held
our legs together & kicked back the sheets
            & warming the milk now i
stand on wooden floor with dreams
of your long hair & that forest again
where our child sits between us
the sun
rolls out
of spoon into eggcup
& i never said that tody
would be as utterly wonderful
or that egg wouldn't run

Martin J. Rosenblum

this winter
fall does not
bleed snow
instead
a belly
full of our love
its heart pumped
blood since summer

this is where

the passion grew
& became the snow
soon on trees
white & clear as nite

watching trees fill
the street with leaves
that hide spring muck

this is when

we roll over
& the bed creaks
in biting morning
air i drove you
to work then go
myself wondering
when it all began
just like this fall

Martin J. Rosenblum

at sunrise (the skin)

icewater hit
a branch by
wind   the tree
laced freezing
snaps from its
         branch
there are stale leaves
scattered on the drifts
            beyond
the shivered tree
      lost
from its branch while i
was sleeping
/at sunrise: fingers
on top of snow, skin is
        the yard

JEROME ROTHENBERG b. 1931

Jerome Rothebnerg was born in Brooklyn ten years after his parents left Poland. *Poland 1931* (New Directions, 1974), from which the following poems were taken, is an attempt "to create through those poems an analogue, a presentation of the Eastern European Jewish world from which I had been cut off by birth, place and circumstance, and to which I no longer have any way of returning, because it doesn't exist in that place any longer. I have gone backward toward an exploration of the reality in general . . . "

He graduated from the City College of New York and received his M.A. from the University of Michigan. The author of over twenty books, he has published many translations of contrmporary German authors. He teaches in the Visual Arts Department of the University of California in San Diego.

Jerome Rothenberg

A POLISH ANECDOTE "THE SAINT"

the man who wouldn't kill an insect
scratched his balls
all day & half the night
would have the rabbi bless his pockets
smiled but never
at a woman   wouldn't even face his wife
but stared out the window
hands behind back he always placed
one foot before the other
remembering the saint who didn't know
his own wife had a wooden leg
until they buried her

A POLISH ANECDOTE "VICTORY"

"he died among colleagues" runs
the Polish epitaph   the body
falls down from the saddle without
sorrow & the other soldiers

ride their horses over him singing
"sleep sleep dear colleague
"in your dark grave
"we wish you sweet dreams about Poland"

beautiful losses etc where each man
has many colleagues only one friend
said Marshal Pilsudski   "to be vanquished &
not to surrender   this is victory!"

Jerome Rothenberg

A GALLERY OF JEWS

a gallery of Jews, love
so perfect it becomes
a solid thing   a person's
or a monster's face made of candles
"if we could only hold the lips
in place" the pink flesh
falls   how beautiful & old
(the women sing) this is no graven image
it is the body of your father
sleeping he was young
he would only wake up to read a book
or smell the rolls
baking in the oven his sisters
cared for
others were walking
in the woods still others
had vanished among the Gentiles
young girls in neckties
riding horses some would buy
magazines with pictures of Polish cities
some wrote to Paris or U.S.A.
& wouldn't eat
Sundays were spent in groups
girls held each other
but spoke of lovers
from the towns   even the young men
sitting on each other's laps
dreamed freedom
on distant walls the wax
was running down
like tears their mothers
wept on Fridays

while waiting for the meat & prunes
still in love
the sisters fitted neatly
into the picture of the perfect town
the young men left for Cuba
farewells
not blessings followed
where they went
the sun way always going down
& shifted
one made a movie   he would dance
his way through life
forgetting his mother's baldness
the virtues that made a woman strong
he fell in love with Gentiles
real blondes were always on his lawn
speaking in German
he would strip down & ride them
psalms burst from his throat
"honkeytonk joys" delivered in a mock accent
he flew westward
to California   no one
wore corsets now
though some forgot how to smile
others would praise him for his teeth
his eyes were ageless
like his clothes
only the pockets changed
the papers faded
walking on country roads at night
still holding hands
the women kept heading toward the towns
old friends had died
along the way to   she could tell you
the exact location of each grave
minutes added up
they would be charged for them in dollars
growing poorer

someone would shuffle the cards
but no one was playing
the photos had slipped into her lap
her glasses fogged
the miracle was that the candle
could keep burning
that there was no one
holding it above his head
to let the wax drip down
the wax had gathered in a metal dish
yellow & pink it sputtered
in the candle's light

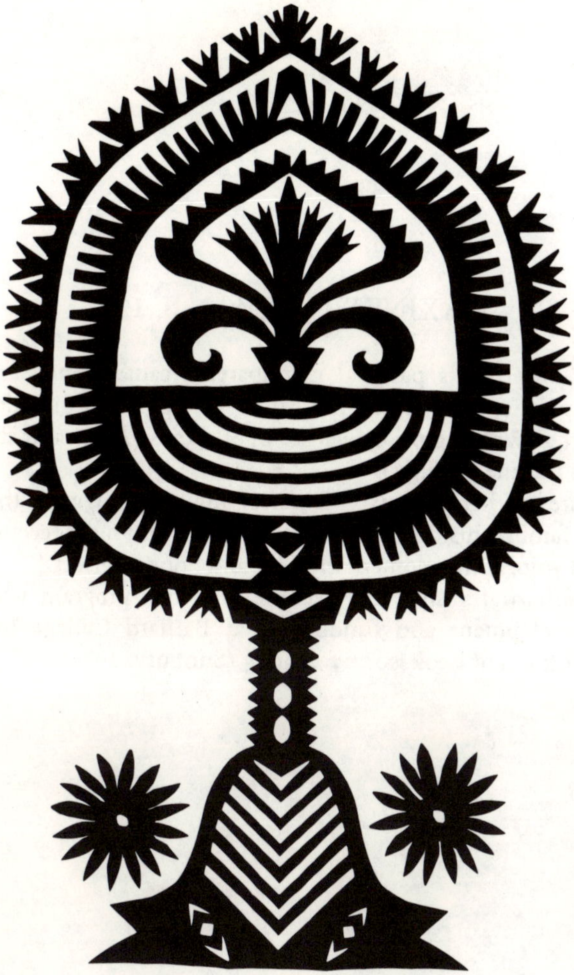

MAXINE SILVERMAN b. 1947

Maxine Silverman's paternal grandparents came from Czestochowa to Sedalia, Missouri to work in the rail yards. She grew up in Sedalia, and she was educated at Washington University in St. Louis (A.B.) and the University of Oregon in Eugene (M.F.A.).

She writes of her poetry: "Some of my work suggests the continuity between my family's history in Eastern Europe and our more recent Midwestern experience. I write at the moment memory and hope intersect."

She administrates an undergraduate academic program which includes curricular development and fundraising at Barnard College in New York City. Her most recent book is *Survival Song* (Sunbury, 1976).

Maxine Silverman

HAIR

Ardently down the backs of cousins
in Poland until it brushed their ribs
the silkworm cousins grew the hair
Sarah Fishoff Silverman peddled
in Missouri.
In Sedalia meager enterprising waves
swelled over coils and switches
off Polish Jews, hair grown
to drape on Sarah's forearm.
She walked the town selling hair
of those who stayed behind,
sticking her other palm out with coins,
trusting strangers to make change
for the hair that caught the fancy
of stylish Midwestern ladies;
the curls and braids that pleased the Nazis
who trimmed their lampshades with Jewish hair,
fashioned bellcords to summon butlers
from my cousins' hair that grew no more.

Maxine Silverman

A COMFORT SPELL

I

My father's teeth gap slightly.
Easy to spit seeds,
a natural grace.

II

"Pa," I write, "I'm low."
"Better soon," he swears. "Soon. Soon.
You're talking to one who knows."

Lord, it's nearly time. October.
He'll pick some leaves off our sugar maples,
pressed, send them to New York.
Flat dry leaves,
and rusty rich.
Pa stays in Missouri,
bets the underdog each tv game,
and the home team, there or away.
"Lord," he whistles through his teeth,
"that boy's a runnin fool. Mercy me."

He names himself:
Patrick O'Silverman,
one of the fightinest!

Melancholy crowds him spring and fall,
regular
seasonal despair,
his brain shocked, his smile fraught with prayer.

I offer what remains of my childhood.
I offer up this comfort spell.

Whoever you are, run in nearly morning
to the center of the park.
There, rooted in the season,
maples send out flame.
Gather to the river the furious leaf.
Mercy
Mercy Buck Up
Mercy Me
Mercy
Mercy Buck Up
Mercy Me

"Pa," I call, "what's new?"
"Nothin much. We're gettin on."

"Pa," I sing, "your leaves came today."
"Oh Maggie," he cries, "just want
to share the fall."

Maxine Silverman

MISSOURI

Missouri.
Here whiles one hawk above prairie.
Scent of heat floats on the absence of breeze.
Among corn, your first horizon, a road
takes the gradual pull and swell of land
in light so tender—
some vanished place you dream and look for.

Farther on, to the north and west,
mountains arrange higher lines.
There are ways that are rivers,
roads beside rivers that fall away
and follow the valley to Creswell.
If there are birds you don't hear any.
Chinook hums on pasture wire,
along pasture and clear fields.
The road extends
so singular
you'll almost regret arriving,
the shout of friends.

BARBARA SZERLIP b. 1949

Barbara Szerlip has never thought of herself as being "Polish-American" but has given much thought of late to her origins, "and in the last few years, my work, without a conscious decision on my part to do so, has become inundated with 'histories'." She writes that her paternal great-grandparents, who spelled their name "Scherlib," came from Rzesziev. Her maternal grandfather's family "claims a descendancy of scholars and rabbis dating back to Elijah Ben Soloman, the Genius of Vilna ('Vilna Goan'), who, at age six, was said to have memorized the Bible."

The recipient of numerous awards, she lives in San Francisco where she edits *Tractor* magazine. Her most recent book is *The Ugliest Woman in the World and Other Histories* (Gallimaufry, 1978).

Barbara Szerlip

Russia, 1931

for Osip Mandelstam

We stand in lines to turn our neighbors in,.
You there, writing poems in the dark.
Do you think you're better? Do any of your verses
put cabbage in the pot?
Wisdom worth having is *cabbage*-wisdom.

What good are poems sewn into cushions
when they come for you in the night
and you can't tell one dream from the other?

Better to weave them, a warm coat for winter.
That would be a wisdom worth having.
Better to stitch them, a passport from this place.
This time. This life.
Or a cow to get you by.

Even the stars are sentries, the moon
a respected informer.

Barbara Szerlip

ENVOY FROM HOUDINI

I knew them better
than they knew themselves
tired of doves and rivers
of silk
I gave them their dreams
to believe in

courted them
with watery inventions
while the band played Asleep
In The Deep

each escape was a kiss
they'd eaten
out their hearts for

I showed them ignorance
like an arm in the sleeve
of their knowledge

Come Back I heard
as if death was a box to unstrap
and climb out of

they kept on begging answers
when the questions
were what fed them and besides
I had given enough

for all my dancing
now they would have me sing

Barbara Szerlip

OPEN LETTER FROM LOLA MONTEZ

the paradox of beauty
is stillness
in the heart of change:
the hurricane's eye
the terrible bell which
lets us forget
that nobody lives forever

wall which we
batlike
bounce our dreams off
candle
on the dim mapless roads

the politics change
but somehow stay the same
'pistols for two and coffee
for one', kingdoms
and soft promises

before it's finished
already it's remembered as a dream

listen
these bones which are dust
twice over
once were flutes

LAURA LOUISE ULEWICZ b. 1930

Laura Louise Ulewicz is a second generation American from Detroit. Her mother knew no English before she started school. "The experience so traumatized her," writes the poet, "that she refused to let me learn Polish. My father's mother gave me clandestine lessons which ended with her death when I was about five." At that point her family moved away from the Polish section, and she had less contact with Polish-Americans.

During the sixties she lived for four years in Europe, spending part of the time in a residential hotel filled with Poles waiting to migrate to the United States. The experience opened up her writing. "Suddenly I was drafting poems which compared their character and life with that of mine, of my grandparents." She has often been told that her poetry has a "Polish tenor" but finds that she "cannot isolate it from the rest of me."

Her collection of poems, *The Inheritance*, published in England by Turret Press, won a Guinness Prize. She currently lives and works in Walnut Grove, California.

Laura Louise Ulewicz

from NOTES TOWARD THE RIVER ITSELF

1

Where the water rises,
again I go, older
and older now; to touch
a little where it rises from
fresh, the quiet, the pool,
tender of our powers;
touch where, inside
the dark, young layers of onion
squeak in older layers.
Always the aging outside
is what shows, arranged
in shawls around the new—
tough protection from
these terrible winds—
as in the cabbage.

5

Light. More light. The weight
of its heat pressing layers
of your flesh down, till hope
is a small dried bird. That's
why the time in the middle
is called an age. It's heat,
light. As if the earth
in the chicken yard flew up
and buzzed in your face. As if
the only breeze came
from the wings of mosquitoes.
Heat, following drought.

So it is that the half-formed
figs thud on the Macadam.
Yet here these round, hot
Chinese pears, flecked
like the bark they are growing on/
from, still hang.
And you're amazed.
Did you think we are spun
between fire and dark
on spits, gutted like game?
We swing through the flame of the sun
sustained by the dark through our navels.
We turn the dark in our minds
like an unripe pear
for a long time before
we let go into it.

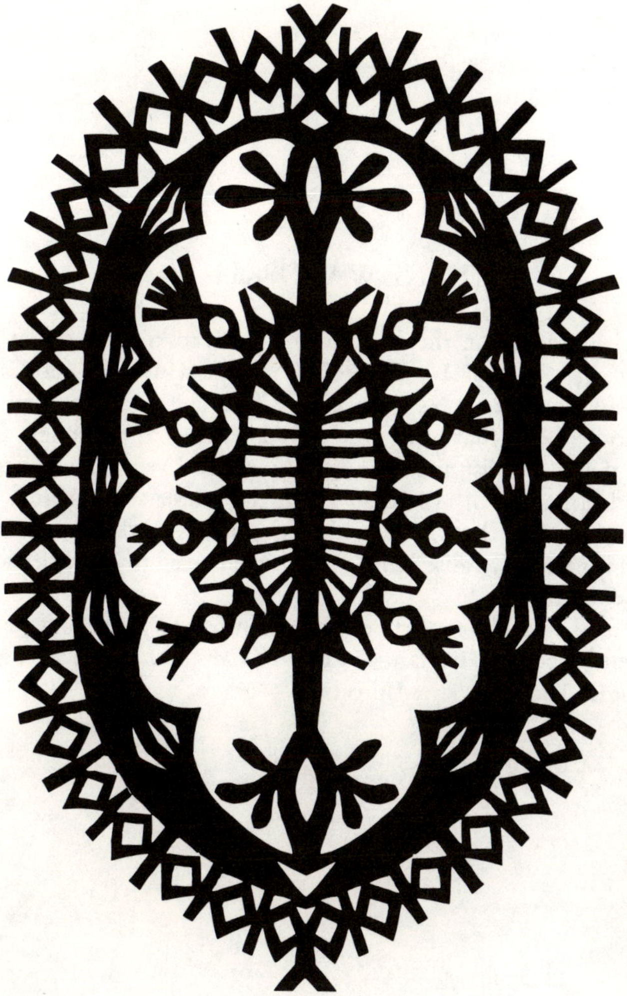

DIANE WAKOSKI b. 1937

Polish influence on the work of Diane Wakoski came rather late in her life. "It wasn't until I graduated from the University of California at Berkeley and moved to New York City and met the poet and translator, Jerome Rothenberg, that I began to have any sense of Polishness at all. And of course that was Polish Jewishness, but it seemed very attractive to me and I began to learn as much as I could about this whole sense of life. Probably, Rothenberg has had the strongest influence on my work of any contemporary poet, and it may be because some part of me allowed that Polish identification to pull me so strongly."

She is one of the most popular contemporary poets, having published some twenty books. Her latest is *Cap of Darkness* (Black Sparrow, 1980). She teaches at Michigan State University.

Diane Wakoski

THE FATHER OF MY COUNTRY

All fathers in Western civilization must have
a military origin. The
ruler,
governor,
yes,
he is
was the
general at one time or other.
And George Washington
won the hearts
of his country—the rough military man
with awkward
sincere
drawing-room manners.

My father;
have you ever heard me speak of him? I seldom
do. But I had a father
and he had military origins—or my origins from
him
are military,
militant. That is, I remember him only in uniform. But of the navy,
30 years a chief petty officer,
always away from home.

It is rough/ hard for me to speak
now.
I'm not used to talking
about him.
Not used to naming his objects/
objects
that never surrounded me.

    A woodpecker with fresh bloody crest
knocks
at my mouth. Father, for the first
time I say
your name. Name rolled in thick Polish parchment scrolls,
name of Roman candle drippings when I sit at my table
alone, each night,
name of naval uniforms and name of
telegrams, name of
coming home from your aircraft carrier,
name of shiny shoes.
name of Hawaiian dolls, name
of mess spoons, name of greasy machinery, and name of
stencilled names.
Is it your blood I carry in a test tube,
my arm,
to let fall, crack, and spill on the sidewalk
in front of the men
I know,
I love,
I know, and
want? So you left my house when I was under two.
being replaced by other machinery (my sister), and
I didn't believe you left me.

                This scene: the trunk yielding treasures of a
                a green fountain pen, heart shaped mirror,
                amber beads, old letters with brown ink, and
                the gopher snake stretched across the palm tree
                in the front yard with woody trunk like monkey
                      skins,
                and a sunset through the skinny persimmon trees.
                    You
                came walking, not even a telegram or post card
                      from
                Tahaiti, Love, love, through my heart like ink in
                the thickest nubbed pen, black and flowing into
                      words

You came, to me, and I at least six. Six doilies
of lace, six battleship cannon, six old beerbottles,
six thick steaks, six love letters, six clocks
running backwards, six watermelons, and six baby
teeth, a six cornered hat on six men's heads, six
lovers at once or one lover at sixes and sevens;
how I confuse
all this with my
dream
walking the tightrope bridge
with gold knots
over
the mouth of an aenemone/ tissue spiral lips
and holding on so that the ropes burned
as if my wrists had been tied

If George Washington
had not
been the Father of my Country
it is doubtful that I would ever have
found
a father. Father in my mouth, on my lips, in my
tongue, out of all my womanly fire,
Father I have left in my steel filing cabinet as a name on my birth
certificate, Father I have left in the teeth pulled out at
dentists' offices and thrown into their garbage cans,
Father living in my wide cheekbones and short feet,
Father in my Polish tantrums and my American speech, Father,
    not a
holy name, not a name I cherish but the name I bear, the name
that makes me one of a kind in any phone book because
you changed it, and nobody
but us
has it,
Father who makes me dream in the dead of night of the falling
    cherry
blossoms, Father who makes me know all men will leave me
if I love them

Father who made me a maverick,
a writer,
a namer,
name/father, sun/father, moon/father, bloody mars/father,

other children said, "My father is a doctor,"
or
"My father gave me this camera,"
or
"My father took me to
the movies,"
or
"My father and I went swimming,"
but
my father is coming in a letter
once a month
for a while,
and my father
sometimes came in a telegram
but
mostly
my father came to me
in sleep, my father because I dreamed in one night that I dug
through the ash heap in back of the pepper tree and found a
    diamond
shaped like a dog, and my father called the dog and it came leaping
over to him and he walked away out of the yard down the road
    with
the dog jumping and nipping at his heels,

my father was not in the telephone book
in my city; my father was not sleeping with my mother
at home;
my father did not care if I studied the
piano;
my father did not care what
I did;

and I thought my father was handsome and I loved him and I
    wondered
why he left me alone so much,
so many years
in fact, but
my father made me what I am,
a lonely woman,
without a purpose, just as I was
a lonely child
without any father. I walked with words, words, and names,
names. Father was not
one of my words.
Father was not
one of my names. But now I say, "George, you have become my
    father
in his 20th century naval uniform. George Washington, I need your
love; George, I want to call you Father, Father, my Father,"
Father of my country,
that is,
me. And I say the name to chant it. To sing it. To lace it around
me like weaving cloth. Like a happy child on that shining afternoon
in the palmtree sunset with her mother's trunk yielding treasures,
I cry and
cry,
Father,
Father,
Father,
have you really come home?

Diane Wakoski

THE SINGER

All songs
are tattoos
on his fingers and toes

As he moves
from year to year
walking on telegrams.

His throat a pipe
is carved with ancient animals;
and telephone wires imitate his hello.

Under his arm
the dream-tortoise struggles
trying to evaporate into the air.

This organ
the red slippery heart
beating in the cushion of each finger
is singu-
lar

a rhythm,
the snow slowly shifting
to cause an avalanche

the dust accumulating
on a window
sill.